Maria Montessori
and her quiet revolution

A picture book about Maria Montessori
and her school method

Written by Nancy Bach
Illustrated by Leo Lätti

Long Bridge Publishing

Maria Montessori and her quiet revolution
A picture book about Maria Montessori and her school method

Text by Nancy Bach
Illustrations by Leo Lätti
Black and white drawings by Julia Norscia
Copyright © 2013 Long Bridge Publishing. All rights reserved.

Find more Italian themed books and biographies at.
www.LongBridgePublishing.com

Publisher's Cataloging in Publication data

Nancy Bach
   Maria Montessori and her quiet revolution / Nancy Bach; illustrated by Leo Lätti
      p.   cm.
   SUMMARY: Illustrated introduction to the life and work of Italian educator Maria Montessori.
Includes historical notes and question pages for readers comprehension review.
   ISBN-13: 978-1-938712-10-4
   ISBN-10: 1-938712-10-2
   1. Montessori, Maria, 1870-1952 --Juvenile literature.   2. Montessori, Maria, 1870-1952.
   3. Montessori method of education --Juvenile literature.   4. Educators.   5. Women --
Biography. 6. Montessori method of education.
   I. Title

Long Bridge Publishing
USA
www.LongBridgePublishing.com

ISBN-13: 978-1-938712-10-4
ISBN-10: 1-938712-10-2

INTRODUCTION

Dr. Maria Montessori was an Italian doctor and educator whose legacy survives in schools bearing her name all over the world. She was born in Italy in 1870 and studied technical subjects, unusual for a woman at the time. She became a Doctor of Medicine, specializing in pediatrics and psychiatry: the first woman to obtain a medical degree in Italy.

Through her work she observed mentally handicapped children and developed methods to educate them far beyond what was thought possible.

She extended her methods to children with normal learning capabilities and established the Montessori approach for educating children in stages from ages 0 to 18. Her method is based on the understanding that children love to play and work together, and do jobs that help them learn. When children leave Montessori schools they know about both school subjects and important life skills.

Dr. Montessori provided training for teachers to open schools in Italy, in other parts of Europe, in the Americas, and in India where she and her son Mario were exiled during World War II.

She lived to the age of 81. She kept working with students and teachers even when she was a very old woman. She spoke to groups around the world to help them support peace instead of war. After her death, her son Mario and her grandchildren kept the Montessori methods going.

Maria's work lives on today, not only in the 20,000 Montessori schools worldwide, but also in public schools and private learning centers where children enjoy programs and activities inspired by her methods.

"Good morning, children. I am your teacher, Mrs. Rinaldi. I am so happy to welcome you to our first day of Montessori school. Please say it with me…Montessori."

Mrs. Rinaldi stood at the front of the room, smiling at the group of young students sitting on the rug before her.
Angela and Brad and the other children mumbled, "Montessori."
"But children, we should say it with pride," said Mrs. Rinaldi. "For that is the name of our founder, Dr. Montessori. Let's try again."

This time Angela and the others raised their voices with their teacher and listened to the name Montessori roll off their tongues.
"Very good. Would you like me to tell you the story of Dr. Montessori?" asked Mrs. Rinaldi.
"Yes," said Angela. "Yes, please," said Susan and Brad.

"Very good!" said the teacher. "I will tell you about a little girl named Maria." "That's my name!" shouted Maria. "Yes. Yes. Maria Montessori was very curious and worked very hard in school. I hope you are that way too, Maria," said Mrs. Rinaldi.

Maria nodded and her curly hair bounced around her head.

"Wonderful. Now children, listen to our story. We'll learn about our founder and understand how our school was started."

Let's go back in time almost 150 years ago, long before cars and computers. In the pretty village of Chiaravalle, in Italy, a little girl was born. Her happy parents named her Maria.

When Maria was five years old her family moved to Italy's capital, Rome, an old and beautiful city. She started school the next year. In those times young girls learned to read and write, but spent much time learning skills like cooking and sewing, which were called "women's work." Maria did well, but she was far more interested in math and science and language.

Because she loved to learn, for middle school, Maria went to a technical school to study challenging subjects. Most girls did not go to technical schools, but Maria did very well! Then, when she was 16, she went to college. There she studied biology, the science of living plants and animals. She found it so interesting that she told her parents, "I want to be a doctor."

Maria's parents were surprised.

At that time, there were no women doctors in Italy or many other parts of the world. Maria was sad when her parents told her that she should become a teacher instead.

Maria felt very strongly that she wanted to be a doctor. What could she do? Whenever she asked permission to go to medical school she was turned away. Maria was smart and a bit stubborn so she did not give up.

Finally she was allowed to attend the School of Medicine at the University of Rome.

Because it was unusual to have a girl at the school, the other students, who were all boys, teased and bullied her. This was difficult for Maria, but she ignored their bullying and just kept studying.

At age 26 she became Italy's first woman doctor. Her parents were very proud.

As a doctor Maria worked with many children who couldn't hear or speak well or had difficulty moving.

She noticed that they learned best when they could do things with their hands and work together. And they had fun, too! Unlike the children in regular schools, who had to sit still for many hours, writing and reading and listening to their teacher.

Back then schools were places with strict rules and no play!

So Maria decided to open her own school and she called it "Children's House."

This school was very different from all the other schools of her time. The furniture was made the right size for young children. Desks were small and chairs were small. There were toys and other objects made of stuff that was fun to touch and they were all put on low shelves that small children could reach. The children didn't have to sit still for many hours. Instead they could learn many activities like cleaning, taking care of pets, and making things. They enjoyed their days at school very much and never felt bored.

Dr. Montessori's school was very successful so she opened many more in Italy, and in other parts of the world, so that many more children could learn and have fun, too.

"And this is why we have our school!" said Mrs. Rinaldi. "What a wonderful gift from Dr. Montessori!" "And now, are you ready to get to work?"

"I am!" said Maria. Angela and Brad and the other children all said "Yes!"

"That's wonderful! I'll show you all the different things we have today and you may pick where you want to start. In our kitchen we are measuring rice. Here is our closet where we are trying on shirts. Our pet hamster needs someone to pet him…" The children looked on as their teacher led them to each exciting new spot in the room.

Each child found a friend and picked a spot to play and work. They were beginning the great new adventure started by a bright and strong-willed little girl, a girl who knew she could do something important even when everyone was telling her "No."

DID YOU KNOW...?

Maria Montessori originally wanted to be an engineer. In the late 1800s there were very few female engineers.

Dr. Montessori learned most of her teaching methods by watching students. She saw what interested them and kept them focused and then put those activities into future lessons. She observed that children were more interested in practical activities (work) than toys (play).

Mario Montessori lived away from his mother while she was busy with her early career. He rejoined Maria when he was fifteen years old and became committed to the Montessori method, acting as his mother's business partner.

Alexander Graham Bell, Thomas Edison, and Helen Keller were all very interested in the Montessori methods.

During World War II, Maria and Mario Montessori lived in India. Mario was interned (put in jail) for two months and Maria was confined to her school because England was at war with Italy. The British people thought that Italians in the British Kingdom and its colonies might be enemies and do something harmful.

Dr. Montessori felt that one role of education of children was reform of society in total and supported "Education for Peace."

Dr. Maria Montessori was nominated for the Nobel Peace Prize three times, in 1949, 1950, and 1951. She was awarded the French Legion of Honor in 1949.

In 1990 Dr. Montessori's face appeared on Italy's 1000 lire banknote with a picture of children working at their studies on the opposite side.

Can you answer these questions?

In which century was Maria Montessori born? 1800 or 1900? ....

What kind of school did she attend? ....

What kind of studies did girls do in Maria Montessori's times?

....

....

Was it easy for her to attend the school of medicine? ....

Why? ....

....

....

What was Maria Montessori's first job? ....

....

What did she observe in that period? ....

....

....

What kind of school did Maria Montessori establish? ....

....

Color and Write

Write the name of 6 things you see in the drawing:

1. _____   4. _____

2. _____   5. _____

3. _____   6. _____

Discover more books about influential people, Italian themed books, and posters!

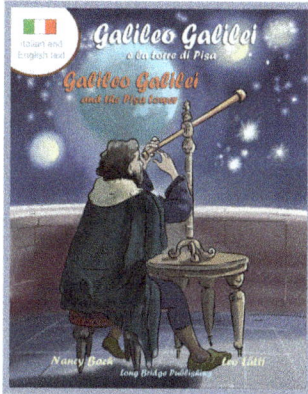
Galileo Galilei e la torre di Pisa / Galileo Galilei and the Leaning Tower
Nancy Back — Leo Lätti
Long Bridge Publishing

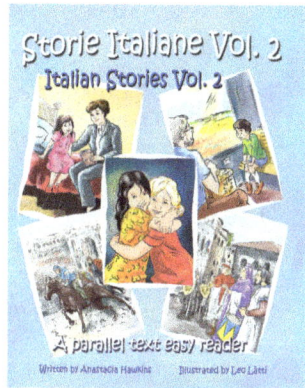
Storie Italiane Vol. 2 / Italian Stories Vol. 2
A parallel-text easy reader
Written by Anastasia Hawkins — Illustrated by Leo Lätti

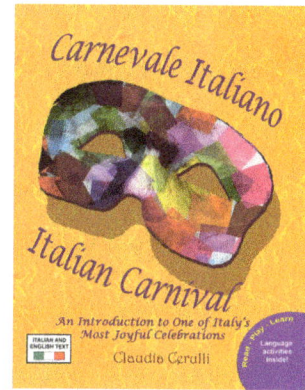
Carnevale Italiano / Italian Carnival
An Introduction to One of Italy's Most Joyful Celebrations
Claudia Cerulli

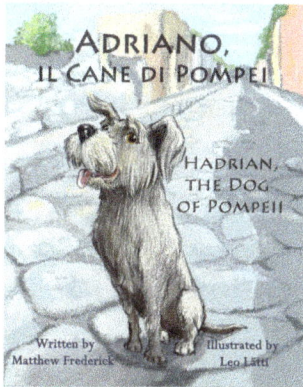
ADRIANO, IL CANE DI POMPEI / HADRIAN, THE DOG OF POMPEII
Written by Matthew Frederick — Illustrated by Leo Lätti

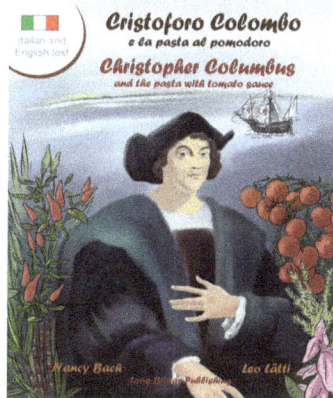
Cristoforo Colombo e la pasta al pomodoro / Christopher Columbus and the pasta with tomato sauce
Nancy Back — Leo Lätti
Long Bridge Publishing

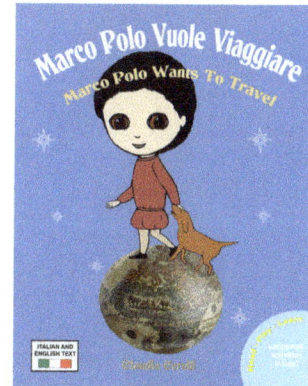
Marco Polo Vuole Viaggiare / Marco Polo Wants To Travel
Claudia Cerulli

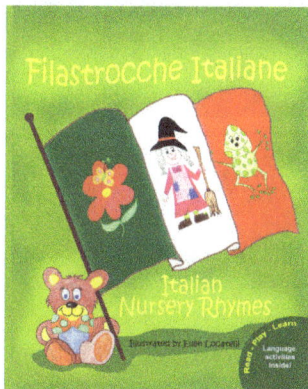
Filastrocche Italiane / Italian Nursery Rhymes
Illustrated by Ester Lucarini

Filastrocche Italiane Vol. 2 / Italian Nursery Rhymes Vol. 2
Illustrated by Julie Weaver

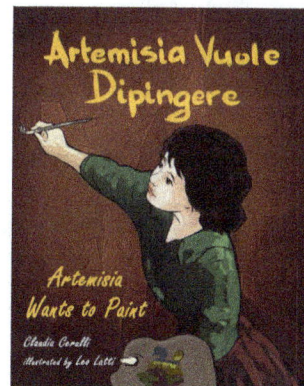
Artemisia Vuole Dipingere / Artemisia Wants to Paint
Claudia Cerulli — Illustrated by Leo Lätti

Visit us online at **www.LongBridgePublishing.com**

9 781938 712104